FIRST ROUTINES

BEDTIME

by Jenna Lee Gleisner

TABLE OF CONTENTS

Words to Know ... 2

Bedtime ... 3

Let's Review! ... 16

Index ... 16

tadpole books

WORDS TO KNOW

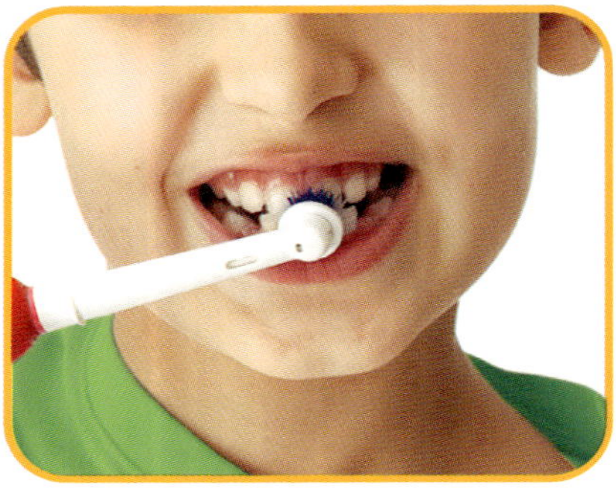

brush

clean

comb

pajamas

read

wash

BEDTIME

I clean up.

I wash my body.

I wash my hair.

pajamas

I put on pajamas.

comb

I comb my hair.

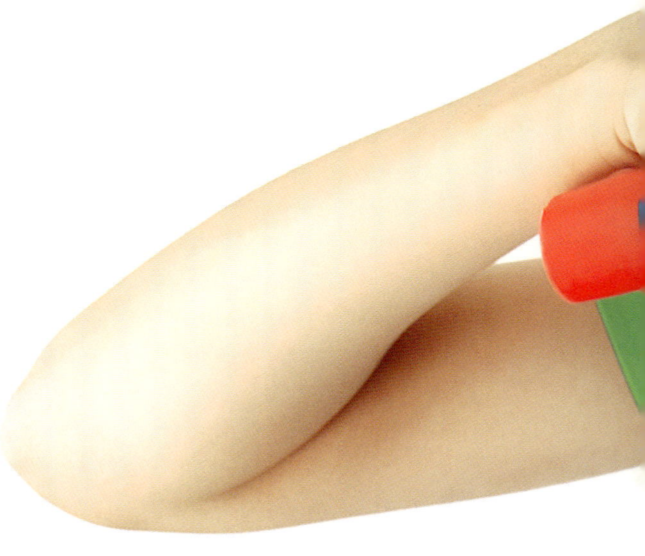

I brush my teeth.

We read a book.

Good night!

LET'S REVIEW!

Which action below is not part of the bedtime routine in the book?

INDEX

body 4
brush 11
comb 9
hair 5, 9
pajamas 7
read 13
teeth 11
wash 4, 5